Lay Servant Ministries

Lay Servant Ministries

Basic Course
Leader's Book

Sandy Jackson with Brian Jackson

DISCIPLESHIP RESOURCES

PO BOX 340003 • NASHVILLE, TN 37203-0003
www.discipleshipresources.org

Cover design by Paul Gant
Interior design by PerfecType

ISBN 13: 978-0-88177-627-0

Printed in the United States of America.

DR 627

Contents

Preface
Thoughts on Teaching and Learning

Each of us has a personal and unique learning style. It may be similar to that of others, but if we are able to use a learning style tailored to the way our brain recognizes, stores, and processes information, learning becomes easy and fun, and information is more effectively retained. Think of how you prefer to learn. Perhaps you are a reader. Maybe you learn more easily and efficiently by listening to music, to other sounds, or to voice. Perhaps you learn best in a "hands-on" manner. If the teaching method suits your learning style, you can process and adapt any information quickly. Addressing the educational needs of all students during a session may require you to modify your presentation style.

While lecture alone is the least effective means of presenting material, group activity is one of the most effective. Relational activities in small groups, or sometimes in the larger class context, associate students with different learning styles and thereby offer a way for the teacher to expose students to multiple avenues of learning. Although some sessions will lend themselves to one or more specific learning styles, the instructor can use a combination to address the needs of the students. As teachers, we need to be creative!

Articles and guidelines concerning multiple intelligences refer to the research of Howard Gardner, or the Multiple Intelligences. These disciplines can be loosely grouped into three categories, or styles: auditory, visual, or tactile (also known as kinesthetic, as it can involve any form of participatory motion or perceived movement). Here are some activity suggestions:

AUDITORY

Class discussion

Music, songs, or rhymes

Show and tell

Poetry, storytelling, and reading

Creative rhythms and raps

Word games

Debate

Seminars

Paraphrase or description

VISUAL

Charts and graphs

Photographs and videos Posters

Timeline and diagrams

Journal writing

Cartoons, bulletin boards

Montages, collages, and collections

TACTILE

Games and simulations Puppets

Construction

Sculpting

Experiments

Drama, dance, and role-playing

Origami and jig-saw puzzles

Signing

Additional help can be obtained in the Train the Trainers section of the *Lay Servant Ministries Guide for Conference and District Committees* available from Discipleship Resources.

Introduction

The *Lay Servant Ministries Basic Course* is an introductory course designed to equip new leaders and renew current leaders. It is the foundational course for the other leadership training courses. This course covers the three main categories of Lay Servant Ministries: Leading, Caring, and Communicating. Each of these categories has its own session and includes material on our Wesleyan heritage. The final session entitled "Into the World" discusses the role of leaders in and beyond the church.

It is important during this course to dispel the notion that lay servants are "preachers." Lay Servant Ministries encompasses a broad range of ministries. Indeed, some persons may have the gifts necessary for preaching, but those who do will learn more about that role in the course on preaching. There are specific courses and processes for filling the role of lay speaker within Lay Servant Ministries. See *The Book of Discipline—2012* or contact your conference or district director of Lay Servant Ministries for more information on this role.

The Basic Course can also be used to prepare new leaders within the congregation of a local church, the church council, etc. In order to give credit to the participants for completing the course and applying toward receiving lay servant credit, the course must be taught as described herein and permission must be received from the district or conference director of Lay Servant Ministries to provide the course for credit. Learning & Leading certificates are available for download at www.gbod.org/laity.

This course was designed to be taught in five two-hour sessions that fulfill the ten-hour course requirement for Lay Servant Ministries. This design is also the preferred format. You may take more time if the study or structure of the academy or school permits, but not less. The session plans have been arranged for the five two-hour sessions format. If the course is taught in a different format, you will need to adjust the session plans.

Participants should have their own copies of the Basic Course so they can take reading notes and complete the biblical reflection material before the course starts. The material suggests outside class assignments to increase the learning outcomes for participants. In the appendix you will find a welcome letter and the first assignment to send to each participant. If leaders teach this course in a weekend format, it will work best if the participants have the book in plenty of time before the course starts, and receive a list of assignments to complete beforehand. The appendix contains a sample letter for use in the weekend format.

As the facilitator of this course, it will be important for you to read the course and become familiar with the material. You may want to have several of the suggested resources available for reference.

NOTE: If you have taught the Basic Course before, you will need to adjust your teaching plans, because this course invites a new approach to Lay Servant Ministries with emphasis on the core categories (Leading, Caring, and Communicating), ministry in daily life, and sharing faith stories. Deviation from the material will lead to inconsistent training and preparation for future courses, mission, and ministries.

Learning Outcomes

Each section of the Basic Course has outcome goals listed for that section. The session plans will enhance the desired learning outcomes.

Resources

You will need a copy of the *Lay Servant Ministries Basic Course Participant's Book*, a copy of *The Book of Discipline* (most recent edition), a Bible, and copies of handouts included in the appendix for various sessions.

Equipment/Materials. The beginning of each session lists necessary materials. A PowerPoint presentation is available for use in leading this course. Download the file at www.gbod.org/laity/lsm-basic_course. You may also use the individual slides with an overhead projector if you do not have computer technology available.

Session Format

Welcome and Devotions. Each session is designed to develop community and provide for Christian conferencing. Please do not skip or forego the opening devotions as sharing worship and prayer is essential to the development of community.

Review of Learning Outcome Goals. It is important to review these goals for each session in order to stay on track during the class sessions.

Topics for Discussion. This part of the class allows for review and discussion opportunities for each of the main topics in a section. **Some discussion topics are designated as small-group activities. These times are also essential for the formation of community.** As leaders, it is important to understand how to facilitate this formation. This is how new leaders will gain experience at leading and using this practice. The participants in each group should change from session to session in order to provide group members with an opportunity to get to know others in the class.

Covenant Groups/Biblical Reflection. This part of the class provides a time of sharing thoughts on the biblical reflections in the book. These groups should remain the same each week to provide a covenant atmosphere and experience. When forming these groups, you may place people from the same church in the same groups, as this may become a nucleus for a covenant group after the session ends. Work to ensure diversity within the group.

Assignments. Before closing, allow time at the end of each session to remind participants of the reading and activity assignments for the next session.

Closing Prayer. Again, this is a time to form community by sharing joys and concerns, committing to pray for those before the next session, and then praying a final prayer together.

Final Session. This is a time of sharing and devotion that concludes the final session. This follows a time of evaluation and discussion of next steps.

Session One
Ministry of the Baptized

LEARNING OUTCOME GOALS

At the end of this session participants will be able to:

1. Describe the reality of the priesthood of all believers and God's call on our lives
2. Discuss spiritual gifts—meaning and purpose
3. Describe the need for a response to God's call
4. Discuss the early Methodist movement and the role of laity in it

EQUIPMENT/RESOURCES

- Flip chart and markers; nametags if not provided by sponsor
- Provide small icons such as crosses (four to six depending on class size, one for each group) each person can hold as he or she speaks. Instruct participants to pass the object to the next person during group discussion times.
- Copies of the devotion and closing prayer for participants (see Session Resources in the appendix)

- Copies of the next session's devotions for volunteers (two to three copies found under the Session Resources section in the appendix)
- *The Faith We Sing* (*TFWS*)
- Bibles for participants who may have forgotten theirs
- *The Book of Discipline* (most recent edition)
- Computer, LCD projector, and screen if using PowerPoint presentation or an overhead projector

Session Plan

INTRODUCTIONS (10 MINUTES)

1. Pass out nametags unless the organization provides them
2. Arrange chairs in a circle, if possible
3. Take the icon or cross, introduce yourself, and share something about yourself. Pass the cross to the next person to do the same. After all the introductions, close with a brief prayer.

WELCOME AND DEVOTIONS (10 MINUTES)

Scripture: 1 Peter 2:9-10
Song: "We Are Marching" (*TFWS* #2235b)
Reading: "Ministry for All"

Who is a "minister"?

Pastors
They practice the *ministry of identity.*

Their work is among believers, as internists in Christ's body.
They are called to teach me about my potential in Christ.

14

I need this ministry to prevent *amnesia*—
that disease of the mind that causes me to forget who I am as a
Christian.

I am a minister too!
I practice the *ministry of vitality*.

My work is in the world, as a farmer, a soldier, an ambassador, I
am called to be salt, light, and leaven in a sick and broken world—
Monday through Saturday.

The world needs this ministry to protect it from anemia—that disease of the blood that slowly robs the system of its health.
All Christians are in *ministry*!

(Pete Hammond, *Lessons, Prayers & Scriptures on the Faith
Journey* [Intervarsity/USA Marketplace], 72.)

Prayer:
I have heard your call to priesthood, my Lord.
I have heard your call to be in mission and ministry.
**Thank you for calling me out of darkness into your marvelous
  light.**
May I declare your praises in all that I am and in all that I do!
Amen.

REVIEW LEARNING OUTCOME GOALS (5 MINUTES)

After review, ask if there are any questions regarding these goals.

TOPICS FOR DISCUSSION

**Ministry of the Baptized/Priesthood of All Believers (5 min-
utes)**

Notes

Notes

Ask the participants to respond to the notion that they are priests/ministers. Show *The Book of Discipline* and give a brief explanation of its purpose.

God's Call and Our Response (20 minutes)

Have participants break into small groups of four to six and briefly discuss their calls and their responses to God using the reflection questions on pages 22 and 23 of the Basic Course Participant's Book.

Spiritual Gifts (15 minutes)

(See pages 16-20 in the Participant's Book)

Discuss the purpose of spiritual gifts. List responses on the flip chart.

Discuss what spiritual gifts are not. List responses on the flip chart.

NOTE: This is not the time to assess spiritual gifts. This can be done in another course or outside the class.

The Role of Laity in Ministry (15 minutes)

(See pages 23-24 in the Participant's Book)

Discuss the examples of lay ministry from early Methodism. How has that activity expanded or decreased in the church today?

Covenant Groups/Biblical Reflection (30 Minutes)

Have participants break into pre-arranged groups. When forming these groups, you may place people from the same church in the same groups, as this may become a nucleus for a covenant group after the session ends. Work to ensure diversity within the group.

Tell participants that these will be their covenant groups throughout the course.

Have participants discuss briefly the biblical reflection questions at the end of session one in the Basic Course Participant's Book, page 24.

ASSIGNMENTS (5 MINUTES)

Read session two in the Basic Course Participant's Book.

Ask participants to observe and make notes on the leadership styles of their current leaders in church, community or workplace.

Ask volunteers to lead the devotion for the next session. Provide copies of suggested format, scripture, song, readings, and prayers found in the appendix.

CLOSING PRAYER (5 MINUTES)

Gather joys and concerns, and then close by praying the following prayer together:

> **Teach me to do your will, for you are my God. Let your good spirit lead me on a level path. Amen** (Ps. 143:10).

Notes

Session Two
Leading

LEARNING OUTCOME GOALS

At the end of this session participants will be able to:

1. Describe servant leadership
2. Discuss the important roles in leadership
3. Describe and discuss what it means to be a spiritual leader
4. Demonstrate the principles of Christian conferencing and describe the aspects of consensus and discernment

EQUIPMENT/RESOURCES

- Flip chart and markers; name tags if not provided by sponsoring organization
- Provide small icons such as crosses (four to six depending on class size, one for each group) each person can hold as he or she speaks. Instruct participants to pass the object to the next person during group discussion times.
- Copies of the devotion and closing prayer for participants
- Copies of next session's devotions for volunteers (two to three copies found in the Session Resources section in the appendix)

Notes

- *The Faith We Sing* (*TFWS*) and/or *The United Methodist Hymnal* (*UMH*)
- Bibles for participants who may have forgotten theirs
- *The Book of Discipline* (most recent edition)
- Computer, LCD projector, and screen if using PowerPoint presentation or an overhead projector

Session Plan

WELCOME AND DEVOTIONS (10 MINUTES)

Be sure to introduce any newcomers who may have missed the first session.

Scripture: John 13:12-17
Song: "Make Me a Servant" (*TFWS* #2176)
Reading:

My God, I lift my face toward you now like a hungry child asking to be fed. My soul is starved; my flesh yearns for the touch that only you can give. Come to me, O God, stay with me; I abandon myself into your hands. Do with me as you will, and whatever you do with me, I thank you. I am prepared for anything; I will accept everything as long as your will is accomplished in the totality of my living.

My God, I give myself to you, placing myself in your hands as a gift of love. It is necessary for me to give myself to you in confidence and without reserve because I love you, and I know you love me also.

Reach down inside me now, O God, and change the gears that race and roar. In place of turmoil give me peace; in place of frenzy give me patience. Then shall I be more like Jesus, who taught us to make room for you in our hectic days.

Teach me, God, to make room for you in all the events and affairs of my days. Then I shall find rest. Then I will be at peace with myself and with you.

(Norman Shawchuck, *A Guide to Prayer for All Who Seek God* [Nashville: Upper Room Books, 2003], 342.)

Prayer: Prayer for a New Heart

Thou who art over us,
Thou who art one of us,
Thou who art.

Give me a pure heart, that I may see thee;
a humble heart, that I may hear thee;
a heart of love, that I may serve thee;
a heart of faith, that I may abide in thee. Amen
(*UMH #392*).

REVIEW LEARNING GOALS (5 MINUTES)

TOPICS FOR DISCUSSION

Spiritual Leadership (20 minutes)

Read the General Rules in *The Book of Discipline*, ¶103. On a flip chart, list the means of grace from page 32 in the Basic Course Participant's Book. Discuss why it is important for leaders to practice these means of grace.

Christian Conferencing (30 minutes)

Divide participants into groups of four to six. Give them one of the situations listed below, and ask them to come to a consensus on a solution using the process on page 40 of the Basic Course Participant's Book.

Notes

Notes

Suggested Topics
1. A leader in the church feels that a new ministry should be started in the community. It will require funding and support from the congregation. Should the church support it?
2. The choir needs new robes. The current ones are shabby, and there are not enough of the right sizes. Should the church buy new ones or try to find some that another church has for sale?
3. A problem has been noted with the conduct of a person in leadership. How should the person be approached about his or her behavior?

A Leader's Role (15 minutes)

Discuss unity of ministry and the developing of new leaders. List ways that laity can work toward unity in ministry by supporting clergy, good communication, and prayer. Keep the discussion positive. This is not a time for clergy or laity bashing. How did participants come to this point in developing their leadership? Was there someone who mentored or encouraged them? List ways they can serve as encouragers or mentors to others.

COVENANT GROUPS/BIBLICAL REFLECTION
(30 MINUTES)

Discuss the questions in the biblical reflection at the end of session two on page 42 in the Basic Course Participant's Book using observations from the last session's assignment.

ASSIGNMENTS (5 MINUTES)

Ask participants to read session three in the Basic Course Participant's Book.

Ask participants to perform an act of compassion and an act of justice before the next session.

Ask for two to three volunteers to lead the devotion for the next session and give them copies of the suggested material.

CLOSING PRAYER (5 MINUTES)

Gather prayer requests and praise reports, and close by praying the following prayer together:

> **Teach me, O Lord, the way of your statutes, and I will observe it to the end.**
>
> **Give me understanding, that I may keep your law and observe it with my whole heart. Amen (Ps. 119:33-34).**

Notes

Session Three
Caring

LEARNING OUTCOME GOALS

At the end of this session participants will be able to:

1. Discuss the biblical basis for caring ministry
2. Compare and contrast acts of compassion and acts of justice
3. Discuss several types of caring ministries
4. Discuss ways to show care for creation

EQUIPMENT/RESOURCES

- Flip chart and markers; name tags if not provided by sponsoring organization
- Provide small icons such as crosses (four to six depending on class size, one for each group) each person can hold as he or she speaks. Instruct participants to pass the object to the next person during group discussion times.
- Copies of the devotion and closing prayer for participants
- Copies of next session's devotions for volunteers (two to three copies found under Session Resources in the Appendix)
- *The United Methodist Hymnal* (*UMH*)

Notes

- Bibles for participants who may have forgotten theirs
- Computer, LCD projector, and screen if using PowerPoint presentation or an overhead projector

Session Plan

WELCOME AND DEVOTIONS (10 MINUTES)

Scripture: Matthew 25:35-37, 40
Song: "Freely, Freely" (*UMH* #389)
Reading: "Privileges"

We **shower daily**, while others bathe in dirty rivers occasionally.
We eat three meals a day, plus unneeded snacks, while others starve.
We sleep warm and soundly while others can never rest.
We have closets filled with unworn clothing, while others wear all they have each day.
We have extended **families**, while others live alone.
We own **homes**, sometimes more than one, while others are homeless.
We enjoy **safety**, while others live with death, war, and violence daily.
We **work** or change jobs, while others beg for minimal survival.
We **travel** extensively and freely, while others live their whole lives where they were born.
We attend **schools** and continuing education, while others suffer illiteracy.
We make and protect **retirement** plans, while others die far too early in poverty.
We have extensive **medical systems**, while others have no health care and die early.

Unlike millions around the world, we North Americans are inordinately blessed, tempted to assume our rights to these gifts, even to fighting for them, and frequently misusing these **privileges** which are on loan from God.

(Pete Hammond, *Lessons, Prayers & Scriptures on the Faith Journey* [Intervarsity/USA Marketplace], 109.)

Prayer:

Lord, forgive my possessive and selfish nature. Help my attempts at becoming a good steward of all the opportunities and gifts that you provide.

Help me to remember and reach out to those without daily bread or the Good News of salvation! Please make me generous like you. Amen.

(Adapted from Pete Hammond, *Lessons, Prayers & Scriptures on the Faith Journey* [Intervarsity/USA Marketplace], 109.)

REVIEW LEARNING OUTCOME GOALS (5 MINUTES)

See page 43 in the Basic Course Participant's Book.

TOPICS FOR DISCUSSION

Works of Mercy: Acts of Compassion and Justice (30 minutes)

On a flip chart, list the acts of compassion and justice that the group performed. Discuss the differences between them (see pages 47 and 48 in the Basic Course Participant's Book).

Caring Ministries (30 minutes)

Divide into small groups and discuss types of caring ministries in each church. Identify ways individuals or congregations can do more to reach out to the community.

Notes

Notes

Stewardship of Creation (20 minutes)

On the flip chart, list ways that we can be good stewards of the earth and other gifts God has given. Discuss making a commitment to practice care of creation. What can we do in our wasteful culture to help improve our environment and the world's natural resources?

COVENANT GROUPS/BIBLICAL REFLECTION (30 MINUTES)

Review the biblical reflection questions on pages 51 and 52 of the Basic Course Participant's Book.

ASSIGNMENTS (5 MINUTES)

Ask participants to read session four in the Basic Course Participant's Book.

Ask participants to come prepared to share their faith story one on one.

Instruct participants to bring a notebook or journal to the next session.

CLOSING PRAYER (5 MINUTES)

Gather prayer requests and close by praying or singing the following prayer together:

Prayer:
For the beauty of the earth, for the glory of the skies,
For the love which from our birth over and around us lies;
> **Lord of all, to thee we raise this our hymn of grateful praise. Amen** (*UMH* #92).

Session Four
Communicating

LEARNING OUTCOME GOALS

At the end of this session participants will be able to:

1. Discuss the importance of communication skills in various settings
2. List the respectful communication guidelines
3. Describe the process of mutual invitation
4. Demonstrate listening skills
5. Share their faith stories with another participant

EQUIPMENT/RESOURCES

- Flip chart and markers; name tags if not provided by sponsoring organization
- Provide small icons such as crosses (four to six depending on class size, one for each group) each person can hold as he or she speaks. Instruct participants to pass the object to the next person during group discussion times.
- Copies of the devotion and closing prayer for participants

Notes

- Copies of the next session's devotions for volunteers (two to three copies found under session resources in the appendix)
- A notebook or journal for participants who may have forgotten theirs
- Computer, LCD projector, and screen if using PowerPoint presentation or an overhead projector

Session Plan

WELCOME AND DEVOTIONS (10 MINUTES)

Scripture: Romans 10:14-15, 17
Song: "To God Be the Glory," verses 1 and 2 (*UMH* #98)
Reading: The Nicene Creed

We believe in one God. The Father, the Almighty, maker of heaven and earth, of all that is, seen and unseen.

We believe in one Lord, Jesus Christ, the Son of God, eternally begotten of the Father, God from God, Light from Light, true God from true God, begotten, not made, of one Being with the Father; through him all things were made.

For us and for our salvation he came down from heaven, was incarnate of the Holy Spirit and the Virgin Mary and became truly human. For our sake he was crucified under Pontius Pilate; he suffered death and was buried. On the third day he rose again in accordance with the scriptures; he ascended into heaven and is seated at the right hand of the Father. He will come again in glory to judge the living and the dead, and his kingdom will have no end.

We believe in the Holy Spirit, the Lord, the giver of life, who proceeds from the Father and the Son, who with the Father and the Son is worshipped and glorified, who has spoken through the prophets. We believe in one holy catholic and apostolic church. We acknowledge one baptism for the forgiveness of sins. We look for the resurrection of the dead, and the life of the world to come. Amen.

Prayer: For God's Reign

> **We believe in you, O God, for you have made the suffering of humanity your suffering. You have come to establish a kingdom of the poor and humble. Today we sing to you, because you are alive, you have saved us, you have made us free. Amen** (*UMBW* #511).

REVIEW LEARNING OUTCOME GOALS (5 MINUTES)

See page 53 in the Basic Course Participant's Book.

TOPICS FOR DISCUSSION

Communication Settings (15 minutes)

Discuss person-to-person communication. Ask participants the following questions:

What is the most important communication setting? What makes it the most important?

What special situations have they experienced (eg. speaking with someone whose native language is different from their own; communication differences between age groups; communication with persons who are mentally challenged)?

Ask all participants to describe their "personal space."

Communication in Small Groups (10 minutes)

Respectful Communication Guidelines (see page 60)

On the flip chart, write the acronym "R-E-S-P-E-C-T" from page 60 in the Basic Course Participant's Book.

Notes

Notes

Have participants fill in the words and discuss why each is important. Ask them to share how they can ensure RESPECT during communication.

Listening Skills (15 minutes)

Have the group discuss listening skills from pages 61-63 in the Basic Course Participant's Book. On the flip chart, list what constitutes a "good" listener and a "poor" listener. Remind participants that they will have the opportunity to practice "good" listening skills as they listen to their partner's faith story.

Communication in Large Assemblies (15 minutes)

Review the key points of addressing large assemblies with the group. Ask participants to suggest some of the skills they have seen used by others for each of the below:

Speech Patterns

Gestures and Body Language

Eye Contact

Humor

Cultural Considerations and Context

Ministry in Daily Life (10 minutes)

1 Peter 3:15 says we should always be ready to give a reason for the hope that lies within us.

Ask the group the question, *Where do you see God at work in your work/school, home, and community?*

How can you join God in that work?

How do people see Jesus in you, your actions, and reactions? Briefly discuss the introduction and sample worksheet Joining God's Mission found in the appendix.

(For more information on Joining God's Mission visit www.gbod.org/laity.)

Sharing Personal Faith Stories (30 minutes)
Divide the group into pairs and share their faith stories with
each other. Have participants evaluate one another's communication and listening skills. Each person has ten minutes to tell
his or her story. After everyone has shared, spend five minutes
evaluating both the speaker and the listener (see Evaluation
Questions on pages 49 and 51 in the appendix).

COVENANT GROUPS/BIBLICAL REFLECTION

Journaling (15 minutes)
Have the group observe quiet time to journal the answers to
the questions found in the Biblical Reflection section on page
68 of the Basic Course Participant's Book. Ask participatnts to
list ways they can make a difference in their daily lives at work,
home, school, or in the community.

ASSIGNMENTS (5 MINUTES)

Ask participants to read session five in the Basic Course
Participant's Book and to find ways to practice hospitality at
church or in a meeting during the week.

CLOSING PRAYERS (5 MINUTES)

Gather joys and concerns and then close by praying the following prayer together:

> **Take my life! Lord, put me to doing your work
> and your will in the world so that the lost and
> hungry souls may be attracted to your love and
> mercy and be drawn into the embrace of your
> love. Amen** (Rueben Job and Norman Shawchuck,
> *A Guide to Prayer for Those Who Seek God*. Nashville:
> Upper Room Books, 2003, 407).

Notes

Session Five
Into the World

LEARNING OUTCOME GOALS

At the end of this session participants will be able to:

1. Describe their roles in fulfilling the Great Commission
2. Discuss the importance of continued study and spiritual growth in the life of Christian leaders
3. Discover the important role of hospitality in the church
4. Briefly describe Appreciative Inquiry and Asset-Based Community Development and discuss ways these tools can be used to spread the gospel

EQUIPMENT/RESOURCES

- Flip chart and markers; nametags if not provided by sponsor
- Provide small icons such as crosses (four to six depending on class size, one for each group) each person can hold as he or she speaks. Instruct participants to pass the object to the next person during group discussion times.
- Copies of the devotion and closing prayer for participants
- *The United Methodist Hymnal* (*UMH*)

Notes

- Computer, LCD projector, and screen if using PowerPoint presentation or an overhead projector

Session Plan

WELCOME AND DEVOTIONS (10 MINUTES)

Scripture: Matthew 28:16-20
Song: "Lead Me, Lord" (*UMH* #473)
Reading: "God's Ways Are Not Our Ways"

We desire pleasure and freedom from pain. God invites us to growth and maturity. We seek escape from difficulty. God encourages us to engage the world's brokenness. We want quick answers to our questions. God asks us to "Be still and know that I am God." We demand solutions to our problems. God teaches life-long learning amid inconvenience, conflict, and pain. We want power and recognition. God calls us to humility. We want relief from stress. God gives us hope in harsh realities. We want safety and security. God beckons us to sacrificial servanthood. We want health and comfort. God offers inner serenity and peace. We want happiness—now. God delivers joy all through life. *"For my thoughts are not your thoughts, Nor are yo ur ways my ways, says the Lord. For as the heavens are higher than the earth, so are my ways higher than yo ur ways, and my thoughts than your thoughts"* (Isaiah 55:8-9).

(Pete Hammond, *Lessons, Prayers & Scriptures on the FaithJourney* [Intervarsity/USA Marketplace], 93.)

Prayer:
God, you are like a baker.
The leaven you provide raises our hopes.
You shape our lives with your hands—they are strong yet gentle.
We ask that you warm us in the oven of your love.

Form our common lives by your grace so that we may in turn nourish hope in the world. We trust in you. Amen.

REVIEW LEARNING OUTCOME GOALS (5 MINUTES)

See page 68 in Basic Course Participant's Book.

TOPICS FOR DISCUSSION

Continuous Study and Spiritual Growth (20 minutes) Discuss the importance of continuous study and the need for spiritual growth as disciples and leaders. None of us have "arrived;" we all are going on to perfection.

List ways that we can continue study—Bible studies, Learning & Leading courses (advanced courses in Lay Servant Ministries), Lay Academies, annual conference session plenaries, and district and annual conference events.

List opportunities for ongoing spiritual growth—intentional practice of the means of grace, covenant/accountable discipleship groups, Walk to Emmaus, Academy for Spiritual Formation (Upper Room), spiritual or prayer retreats, and days apart.

Discuss possibilities in arranging days apart. Is this possible? Should time apart with God be a priority?

Notes

Notes

Hospitality (20 minutes)

Have the group divide into smaller groups and discuss their experiences practicing hospitality both in the church and at meetings per their assignment from last session.

What were their experiences?

What difference does it make, both to the other persons and to themselves?

Appreciative Inquiry and Asset-Based Community Development (30 minutes)

Discuss how looking at assets and positive experiences rather than focusing on a lack of resources or negative experiences could change the way we plan and evaluate ministries. How might the outlook regarding our opportunities change?

Discuss organizations in the community that might become partners in mission and ministry. How could our mission and ministry expand if we join resources with other churches or community organizations?

How can we work together to care for God's people and promote the kingdom of God on earth?

COVENANT GROUPS / BIBLICAL REFLECTION (20 MINUTES)

Review questions from the biblical reflection on page 78 of the Basic Course Participant's Book.

FINAL SESSION

Wrap-Up (5 minutes)

Review next steps for Lay Servant Ministries.

Closing (10 minutes)

Centering Prayer:

> Like the sun that is far away and yet close at hand to warm us, so God's spirit is ever present around us.
>
> Come, Creator, into our lives. We live and move and have our very being in you. Open now the windows of our souls. Amen (from *1987 United Methodist Clergywomen's Consultation Resource Book*, 61).

Song: "Here I am, Lord" (*UMH #593*)

Closing Prayer: A Covenant Prayer in the Wesleyan Tradition

I am no longer my own, but thine.
Put me to what thou wilt, rank me with whom thou wilt.
Put me to doing, put me to suffering.
Let me be employed by thee or laid aside for thee,
exalted for thee, or brought low for thee.
Let me be full, let me be empty.
Let me have all things, let me have nothing.
I freely and heartily yield all things
to thy pleasure and disposal.
And now, O glorious and blessed God,
Father, Son, and Holy Spirit,
thou art mine and I am thine. So be it.
And the covenant which I have made on earth,
Let it be ratified in heaven. Amen.

Notes

Notes

_____

_____

_____

_____

_____

_____

_____

_____

_____

_____

_____

_____

_____

_____

_____

_____

_____

_____

_____

_____

Sharing Signs of Peace

Blessing: Sarum Blessing

God be in your head, and in your understanding. God be in your eyes, and in your looking.

God be in your mouth, and in your speaking. God be in your heart, and in your thinking.

God be at your end, and at your departing. Amen (*UMBW* #566).

Appendix

Participant's Letter
(Five Sessions)

Dear Participant,

Welcome to the Basic Course in Lay Servant Ministries. You are about to enter into a commitment to quality biblical leadership. Lay Servant Ministries presents a broad range of mission and ministry opportunities. The Basic Course is the foundational course which lays the framework for all leadership in mission and ministry. Each course will equip leaders to better lead and work with others, not only in the church, but also in the community and throughout the world.

In the Basic Course, topics such as servant and spiritual leadership, caring ministries, basic communication skills, sharing your faith, and leading meetings will enhance your knowledge and skill as a leader.

This course is not designed to prepare you to preach. Those who have gifts for preaching may take the advanced course on preaching after this course.

There will be five, two-hour sessions. Please plan to attend all of the sessions; missing any will leave a hole in the group and lessen the experience for you and others.

The sessions are scheduled:

Dates: _____

Time: _____

Location: _____

Notes

Before the first session, please read session one and the biblical reflection. Take notes and list questions you have so that they can be clarified in class.

Find a copy of the most recent edition of *The Book of Discipline*. Read ¶104 if possible before the first session. You may be asked to volunteer to lead the devotions in one of the sessions. Devotions have already been prepared for you to use.

Bring your Bible and a notebook or journal to each class, along with your copy of the Basic Course.

Come with a willingness to learn what God has in store for you as a leader. Bring a positive attitude and be ready to participate in the discussions both in the large group and in small groups. One of the best ways to learn is through the experiences of others.

You will participate as a member of a covenant group throughout the class. This experience will give you an idea of the potential for deep sharing that is possible in this type of small group.

I am praying for you and look forward to our time together. In ministry together,

(signature)

Participant's Letter (Weekend Session)

Dear Participant,

Welcome to the Basic Course in Lay Servant Ministries. You are about to enter into a commitment to quality biblical leadership. Lay Servant Ministries presents a broad range of mission and ministry opportunities. The Basic Course is the foundational course that lays the framework for all leadership in mission and ministry. Each course will equip leaders to better lead and work with others, not only in the church, but also in the community and throughout the world.

In the Basic Course, topics such as servant and spiritual leadership, caring ministries, basic communication skills, sharing your faith, and leading meetings will enhance your knowledge and skill as a leader.

This course is not designed to prepare you to preach. Those who have gifts for preaching may take the advanced course on preaching after this course.

(The date, time, and location where the class is scheduled)

Before the class, please read sessions one through five along with the biblical reflections. Take notes and list questions you have so that they can be clarified in class.

Please complete these assignments before class:

Notes

1. Find a copy of the most recent edition of the *The Book of Discipline*. Read ¶104 if possible before the class starts.

2. Observe and make notes on the leadership styles of your leaders (past or present) in church, community, or workplace.

3. Perform an act of compassion and an act of justice and be ready to describe them, their effects on you, and any potential or realized influence on the recipients.

4. Come prepared to share your faith story with one other person in the group.

5. Find ways to practice hospitality at church or during a meeting, and be prepared to discuss the effect on you and on the people who received your hospitality.

You may be asked to volunteer to lead the devotions in one of the sections of the course. Devotions have been prepared for you to use.

Bring your Bible and a notebook or journal to each class along with your copy of the Basic Course.

Come with a willingness to learn what God has in store for you as a leader, have a positive attitude, and be ready to participate in the discussions both in the large group and in small groups. One of the best ways to learn is through the experiences of others.

You will participate as a member of a covenant group throughout the class. This experience will give you an idea of the potential for deep sharing that is possible in this type of small group.

I am praying for you and look forward to our time together,

(signature)

Sample Christian Conferencing Format

Sing or read the hymn "Sanctuary" (*TFWS* #2164)

Scripture: Hebrews 10:24-25
"And let us consider how we may spur one another on toward love and good deeds. Let us not give up meeting together, as some are in the habit of doing, but let us encourage one another . . ."

Responsive Reading: "Cry of My Heart"
Leader: It is the cry of my heart
ALL: to follow you.
Leader: It is the cry of my heart
ALL: to be close to you.
Leader: It is the cry of my heart
All: to follow all of the days of my life.
Leader: Teach me your holy ways, O Lord
ALL: so I can walk in your truth.
Leader: Teach me your holy ways, O Lord
All: and make me wholly devoted to you.
Leader: Open my eyes so I can see

Notes

ALL: the wonderful things that you do.
Leader: Open my heart up more and more
ALL: and make me wholly devoted to you.

Gather Prayer Concerns

Prayer (*UMH #335*)
O God, the Holy Spirit, come to us and among us,
Come as the wind and cleanse us, come as the fire and burn, Come as the dew and refresh.
Convict, convert, and consecrate many hearts and lives to our great good and to Thy greater glory. And this we ask for Jesus Christ's sake. Amen.

CLOSING
Hymn: "Lord, Be Glorified" (*TFWS #2150*)

A Covenant Prayer in the Wesleyan Tradition (*UMH #607*)
I am no longer my own, but thine.
Put me to what thou wilt, rank me with whom thou wilt.
Put me to doing, put me to suffering.
Let me be employed by thee or laid aside for thee,
Exalted for thee or brought low for thee.
Let me be full, let me be empty.
Let me have all things, let me have nothing.
I freely and heartily yield all things
to thy pleasure and disposal.
And now, O glorious and blessed God,
Father, Son, and Holy Spirit,
thou art mine, and I am thine. So be it.
And the covenant which I have made on earth,
let it be ratified in heaven. **Amen.**

Evaluation Questions

Did the listener make eye contact without staring?   Yes   No

Did the listener nod, smile, or use other facial expressions to
indicate that he or she was listening?   Yes   No

Did the listener interrupt you?   Yes   No

Did the listener appear closed to what you were saying?   Yes   No

Positive comments for the listener:

Suggestions for the listener:

Evaluation Questions

Did the speaker maintain your personal space?   Yes   No

Did the speaker understandable?   Yes   No

Did the story flow well?   Yes   No

Did the story seem disorganized and difficult to follow?   Yes   No

Did the speaker look at you while he or she was talking?   Yes   No

Did the speaker use annoying or distracting gestures or
speech patterns?   Yes   No

Positive comments for the speaker:

Suggestions for the speaker:

Session Resources

(Available for download at www.gbod.org/laity)

Session One

DEVOTION

Scripture: 1 Peter 2:9-10
Song: "We Are Marching" (*TFWS* #2235b)
Reading: "Ministry for All"

Who is a "minister"?
Pastors
They practice the *ministry of identity*.
Their work is among believers, as internists in Christ's body. They are called to teach
me about my potential in Christ. I need this ministry to prevent *amnesia*—
that disease of the mind that causes me to forget who I am as a Christian.
I am a minister too!
I practice the *ministry of vitality*.
My work is in the world, as a farmer, a soldier, an ambassador,
I am called to be salt, light, and leaven in a sick and broken world— Monday
through Saturday.

Notes

The world needs this ministry to protect it from *anemia*—
that disease of the blood that slowly robs the system of its health.
All Christians are in *ministry*!

(Pete Hammond, *Lessons, Prayers & Scriptures on the Faith Journey*
[Intervarsity/USA Marketplace], 72.)

Prayer:
I have heard your call to priesthood, my Lord.
I have heard your call to be in mission and ministry.
**Thank you for calling me out of darkness into your marvel-
ous light. May I declare your praises in all that I am and
in all that I do! Amen.**

CLOSING PRAYER

Teach me to do your will, for you are my God.
Let your good spirit lead me on a level path.
Amen (Ps. 143:10).

Session Two

Scripture: John 13:12-17
Song: "Make Me a Servant" (*TFWS* #2176)
Reading:

> My God, I lift my face toward you now like a hungry child asking to be fed. My soul is starved; my flesh yearns for the touch that only you can give. Come to me, O God, stay with me; I abandon myself into your hands. Do with me as you will, and whatever you do with me, I thank you. I am prepared for anything; I will accept everything as long as your will is accomplished in the totality of my living.
>
> My God, I give myself to you, placing myself in your hands as a gift of love. It is necessary for me to give myself to you in confidence and without reserve because I love you, and I know you love me also.
>
> Reach down inside me now, O God, and change the gears that race and roar. In place of turmoil give me peace; in place of frenzy give me patience. Then shall I be more like Jesus, who taught us to make room for you in our hectic days.
>
> Teach me, God, to make room for you in all the events and affairs of my days. Then I shall find rest. Then I will be at peace with myself and with you (Rueben Job and Norman Shawchuck, *A Guide to Prayer for All Who Seek God* [Nashville: Upper Room Books, 2003], 342).

Notes

_____
_____
_____
_____
_____
_____
_____
_____
_____
_____
_____
_____
_____
_____
_____
_____
_____
_____

Prayer: "Prayer for a New Heart"
Thou who art over us,
Thou who art one of us, Thou who *art*:
    Give me a pure heart, that I may see thee;
      a humble heart, that I may hear thee;
      a heart of love, that I may serve thee;
      a heart of faith, that I may abide in thee. Amen
(*UMH* #392).

CLOSING PRAYER

Teach me, O Lord, the way of your statutes, and I will
    observe it to the end.
Give me understanding, that I may keep your law
and observe it with my whole heart. Amen (Ps. 119:33-34).

Session Three

Scripture: Matthew 25:35-37, 40
Song: "Freely, Freely" (*UMH* #389)
Reading: "Privileges"

We **shower daily**, while others bathe in dirty rivers occasionally.
We eat three meals a day, plus unneeded snacks, while others starve.
We sleep warm and soundly while others can never rest.
We have closets filled with unworn clothing, while others wear all they have each day.
We have extended **families,** while others live alone.
We own **homes,** sometimes more than one, while others are homeless.
We enjoy **safety,** while others live with death, war, and violence daily.
We **work** or change jobs, while others beg for minimal survival.
We **travel** extensively and freely, while others live their whole lives where they were born.
We attend **schools** and continuing education, while others suffer illiteracy.
We make and protect **retirement** plans, while others die far too early in poverty.
We have extensive **medical systems**, while others have no health care and die early.
Unlike millions around the world, we North Americans are inordinately blessed, tempted to assume our rights to these gifts, even to fighting for them, and frequently misusing these **privileges** which are on loan from God.

(Pete Hammond, *Lessons, Prayers & Scriptures on the Faith Journey* [Intervarsity/USA Marketplace], 109.)

Notes

Prayer:

Lord, forgive my possessive and selfish nature. Help my attempts at becoming a good steward of all the opportunities and gifts that you provide.

Help me to remember and reach out to those without daily bread or the Good

News of salvation! Please make me generous like you. Amen.

(Adapted from Pete Hammond, *Lessons, Prayers & Scriptures on the Faith Journey* [Intervarsity/USA Marketplace], 109.)

CLOSING PRAYER

For the beauty of the earth, for the glory of the skies,
For the love which from our birth, over and around us lies;
Lord of all, to thee we raise this our hymn of grateful praise. Amen (*UMH #92*).

Session Four

Scripture: Romans 10:14-15, 17
Song: "To God Be the Glory," verses 1 and 2 (*UMH* #98)
Reading: The Nicene Creed

> We believe in one God, the Father, the Almighty, maker of heaven and earth, of all that is, seen and unseen.
>
> We believe in one Lord, Jesus Christ, the Son of God, eternally begotten of the Father, God from God, Light from Light, true God from true God, begotten, not made, of one Being with the Father; through him all things were made.
>
> For us and for our salvation he came down from heaven, was incarnate of the Holy Spirit and the Virgin Mary and became truly human. For our sake he was crucified under Pontius Pilate; he suffered death and was buried. On the third day he rose again in accordance with the scriptures; he ascended into heaven and is seated at the right hand of the Father. He will come again in glory to judge the living and the dead, and his kingdom will have no end.
>
> We believe in the Holy Spirit, the Lord, the giver of life, who proceeds from the Father and the Son, who with the Father and the Son is worshipped and glorified, who has spoken through the prophets. We believe in one holy catholic and apostolic church. We acknowledge one baptism for the forgiveness of sins. We look for the resurrection of the dead, and the life of the world to come. Amen.

Notes

Prayer: For God's Reign

We believe in you, O God, for you have made the suffering of humanity your suffering. You have come to establish a kingdom of the poor and humble. Today we sing to you, because you are alive, you have saved us, you have made us free. Amen (*UMBW* #511).

Closing Prayer

Take my life! Lord, put me to doing your work and your will in the world so that the lost and hungry souls may be attracted to your love and mercy and be drawn into the embrace of your love. Amen (Reuben Job and Norman Shawchuck, *A Guide to Prayer for Those Who Seek God*, [Nashville: Upper Room Books, 2003], 407).

Session Five

Scripture: Matthew 28:16-20
Song: "Lead Me Lord" (*UMH* #473)
Reading: God's Ways Are Not Our Ways

We desire pleasure and freedom from pain. God invites us to
growth and maturity. We seek escape from difficulty.
God encourages us to engage the world's brokenness.
We want quick answers to our questions.
God asks us to "Be still and know that I am God." We demand
solutions to our problems.
God teaches life-long learning amid inconvenience, conflict, and pain.
We want power and recognition.
God calls us to humility. We want relief from stress.
God gives us hope in harsh realities.
We want safety and security.
God beckons us to sacrificial servanthood.
We want health and comfort. God offers inner serenity and peace.
We want happiness—now.
God delivers joy all through life. *"For my thoughts are not your*
thoughts, Nor are yo ur ways my ways, says the Lord.
For as the heavens are higher than the earth, so are my ways higher
than your ways, and my thoughts than your thoughts"
(Isaiah 55:8-9).

(Pete Hammond, *Lessons, Prayers & Scriptures on the Faith Journey*
[Intervarsity/USA Marketplace], 93.)

Notes

Prayer:

God, you are like a baker.

The leaven you provide raises our hopes.

You shape our lives with your hands—they are strong yet gentle. We ask that you warm us in the oven of your love.

Form our common lives by your grace so that we may in turn nourish hope in the world. We trust in you. Amen.

CLOSING WORSHIP

Centering Prayer:

Like the sun that is far away and yet close at hand to warm us, so God's spirit is ever present around us.

Come, Creator, into our lives. We live and move and have our very being in you.

Open now the windows of our souls. Amen (*1987 United Methodist Clergywomen's Consultation Resource Book*, 61).

Song: "Here I am, Lord" (*UMH* #593)

Closing Prayer: A Covenant Prayer in the Wesleyan Tradition (*UMH* #607)

I am no longer my own, but thine.

Put me to what thou wilt, rank me with whom thou wilt.

Put me to doing, put me to suffering.

Let me be employed by thee or laid aside for thee,

exalted for thee, or brought low for thee.

Let me be full, let me be empty.

Let me have all things, let me have nothing.

I freely and heartily yield all things

to thy pleasure and disposal.

And now, O glorious and blessed God,

Father, Son, and Holy Spirit,

Thou art mine and I am thine. So be it.

And the covenant which I have made on earth,
Let it be ratified in heaven. Amen.

Sharing Signs of Peace

Blessing: Sarum Blessing
God be in your head, and in your understanding. God be in
your eyes, and in your looking.
God be in your mouth, and in your speaking. God be in
your heart, and in your thinking.
God be at your end, and at your departing.
Amen (*UMBW* #566).

Notes

Introduction to Joining God's Mission

The reality is that many baptized Christians do not understand the impact their daily lives can have on the world. They tend to think of mission or ministry as something that the church does, specifically the clergy. Or their understanding of ministry refers only to those things that happen within the context of the church.

Another reality is the disconnect that occurs between Sunday and Monday because the church is not connecting Christians to their daily lives in specific ways.

Early Methodists understood their role in society and were equipped through class meetings for those roles. Joining God's Mission is an attempt to enable laity and clergy to consider their everyday lives areas of mission and to seek support for this mission in a covenant setting.

The congregation can support and equip this effort by attentiveness to raising daily-life ministry or mission as valid, and by providing the means for laity to develop this understanding and become equipped to join God's mission in the world.

Joining God's Mission is not another church program—it is a way of BEING the church that impacts the world!

Daily Mission 1

(The Daily Mission worksheets are available for download
at www.gbod.org/laity)

Joining God's Mission in the Workplace or School

Where is God at work in my workplace or school? How can I join God in that work? "I believe God is . . ."

What is my vision for how I can make a difference in my work or school life? What am I doing now to make that vision a reality? Where can I improve?

What are the specific actions I will take to reach this vision?

Works of Piety

Acts of Devotion

Acts of Worship

Works of Mercy: Acts of Compassion

Acts of Justice

Who will help hold me accountable for this ministry?

CPSIA information can be obtained
at www.ICGtesting.com
Printed in the USA
LVOW05s0247010416

481668LV00005B/27/P

9 780881 776270